GEARING UP FOR SPORTS!

BASEBALL GEAR

NOAH RICCARDI

PowerKiDS press

Published in 2027 by The Rosen Publishing Group, Inc.
2544 Clinton Street, Buffalo, NY 14224

First Edition

Book Design: Madison Thogmartin

Photo Credits: Cover, p. 1 mTaira/Shutterstock.com; p. 5 Lane V. Erickson/Shutterstock.com; p. 7 Rick Scuteri/Shutterstock.com; p. 9 JoeSAPhotos/Shutterstock.com; p. 11 James Stuart Griffith/Shutterstock.com; p. 13 Jon Osumi/Shutterstock.com; p. 15 Al Ungar/Shutterstock.com; p. 17 Michael Rolands/Shutterstock.com; p. 19 Conor P. Fitzgerald/Shutterstock.com; p. 21 PeopleImages/Shutterstock.com.

Cataloging-in-Publication Data
Names: Riccardi, Noah.
Title: Baseball gear / Noah Riccardi.
Description: Buffalo, New York : PowerKids Press, 2027. | Series: Gearing up for sports! | Includes glossary and index.
Identifiers: ISBN 9781499456615 (pbk.) | ISBN 9781499456622 (library bound) | ISBN 9781499456639 (ebook)
Subjects: LCSH: Baseball--Juvenile literature. | Baseball--Equipment and supplies--Juvenile literature.
Classification: LCC GV867.5 R533 2027 | DDC 796.357--dc23

Manufactured in China

CPSIA Compliance Information: Batch #QS27PK. For Further Information contact Rosen Publishing, at 1-800-237-9932.

CONTENTS

The Ball

Every baseball game needs a ball. A baseball is round and about 3 inches (7.62 cm) wide. It is white with red **stitching**. The ball is hard. It bounces less than balls in other sports.

Teams made early baseballs by hand. In the 1800s, the ball's size and weight changed from game to game. Then teams made rules to keep balls the same for every team. Workers still stitch baseballs by hand today.

The Bat

Players hit the ball with the bat. The bat's **handle** is thin. The **barrel** is thicker. The best spot to hit the ball is the middle of the barrel. This is called the sweet spot.

Bats can use different **materials**. In Little League, high school, and college baseball, players use metal bats. Pro players use wooden bats. Wooden bats can be made from maple, ash, or birch trees.

The Glove

Fielders use gloves to catch the ball. Gloves are made of leather. They protect the fielder's hand. Fans also bring their own gloves to stadiums to catch balls that leave the field.

Some positions use special gloves. The first baseman uses a very wide glove. This makes it easier to catch balls thrown by teammates. The catcher wears a glove with thick padding. This protects their hand while catching fast pitches.

Cleats

Players wear shoes with spikes on the bottom. These shoes are called cleats. Cleats grip the ground. They make it easier to run on grass or dirt without slipping.

Batter's Protection

Fast pitches can be dangerous, so the batter needs equipment so they can stay safe. The batter wears a helmet to protect their head. Some batters also use pads to protect their elbow and **shin**.

Catcher's Gear

Pitches can also hit the catcher. To avoid **injuries**, the catcher wears a helmet and mask over their face. The catcher also wears shinpads on their legs. A shield protects their chest.

GLOSSARY

barrel: The thickest part of the bat.

fielders: The players who try to catch the ball on defense.

handle: The part of the bat that a player holds.

injuries: When a player gets hurt during a game.

materials: What things are made of.

shin: The front of the lower part of the leg.

stitching: Thread woven into the baseball to hold it together.

FOR MORE INFORMATION

BOOKS

Abdo, Kenny. *Baseball GOATs*. Minneapolis, MN: Abdo Publishing, 2025.

Leed, Percy. *Pro Baseball by the Numbers*. Minneapolis, MN: Lerner Publications, 2025.

WEBSITES

Britannica Kids: Baseball
kids.britannica.com/kids/article/baseball/352829
Learn more about baseball rules and gameplay.

Sports Illustrated: Batter Up
blog.library.si.edu/blog/2016/07/13/summertime-sports-early-twentieth-century-baseball-equipment/
See how baseball equipment used to look.

Publisher's note to educators and parents: Our editors have carefully reviewed these websites to ensure that they are suitable for students. Many websites change frequently, however, and we cannot guarantee that a site's future contents will continue to meet our high standards of quality and educational value. Be advised that students should be closely supervised whenever they access the internet.

INDEX